INSPIRATION FOR *Life's*

RELATIONSHIPS

Quotations from Mary Baker Eddy

INSPIRATION FOR

Life's

RELATIONSHIPS

Quotations from Mary Baker Eddy

THE WRITINGS OF **MaryBakerEddy**

BOSTON

Compilation and new material © 2002 The Writings of Mary Baker Eddy

Compiled by F. Lynne Bachleda
DESIGN BY PRESSLEY JACOBS: a design partnership

Publisher's Cataloging-in-Publication

Eddy, Mary Baker, 1821-1910.
    Inspiration for life's relationships : quotations from
  Mary Baker Eddy. — 1st ed.
  p. cm.
  LCCN 2002113910
  ISBN 0-87952-276-3

  1. Eddy, Mary Baker, 1821-1910 — Quotations.
2. Spiritual Life — Christianity — Quotations, maxims, etc.
I. Title.

BX6941.I57 2002   289.5'2

* table of contents *

preface

*O*ur relationships shape us even as we shape them. Our dialogue within ourselves, our interactions at home, at work, in the world — our connection with God — form the surround for our journey through life. For both introspection and discussion, this book is a wellspring of inspiration, comfort and encouragement for all of life's relationships.

Mary Baker Eddy, whose writings are the source for these pages, has been a mentor and counselor to many. Her wisdom is born of rich life experience. Her encouragement — fortified by spiritual understanding — strengthens and comforts in moments of need. Her compassion — from the love that fueled all her work — points to the connection we all have with God.

The wisdom, encouragement and compassion of Mary Baker Eddy's words flow from a lifetime of spiritual searching and of caring deeply about the people around her. Her girlhood, in the early 1800s, was marked by the unfailing love of a devout mother, the sometimes-harsh pronouncements of a more rigid father, and a strong faith in God's presence. She moved within an active circle of friends, older siblings, and many suitors. Even with the limitations that every woman of her time faced, Mary had hopes for a promising future.

Circumstances were not kind, however. The early deaths of a favorite brother, her beloved mother and her newlywed husband along with struggles for physical health and financial security brought grief, weakness and isolation to Mary's adulthood. But her faith in God never left her. At the point of deepest incapacity due to a life-threatening injury, Mary made the discovery that transformed her life. Her prayers led to a period of spiritual clarity that both healed her body and moved her from isolation to a vision universal in scope. She discovered the spiritual law of God's absolute, unwavering love.

The power of this discovery, combined with Mary Baker Eddy's natural regard for all humanity, impelled her to think far beyond her own neighborhood. She soon embarked on what would become a forty-four year mission of sharing what she'd learned about God through healing, writing, publishing and teaching.

She wrote a book about her discovery, *Science and Health with Key to the Scriptures*, many passages of which are quoted in this volume. Millions of people around the world have read this book and been touched — and healed — by its ideas.

As you explore these pages, take a moment to savor what you find. The ideas will intrigue you, move you, comfort you. For those already acquainted with Mary Baker Eddy, it's a quiet exploration with a long-time friend — someone you know very well, but whose thoughts still have the ability to inspire you. For those just beginning a conversation with this remarkable author, teacher and healer, link arms with her on an inspiring adventure of discovery.

CHAPTER

1

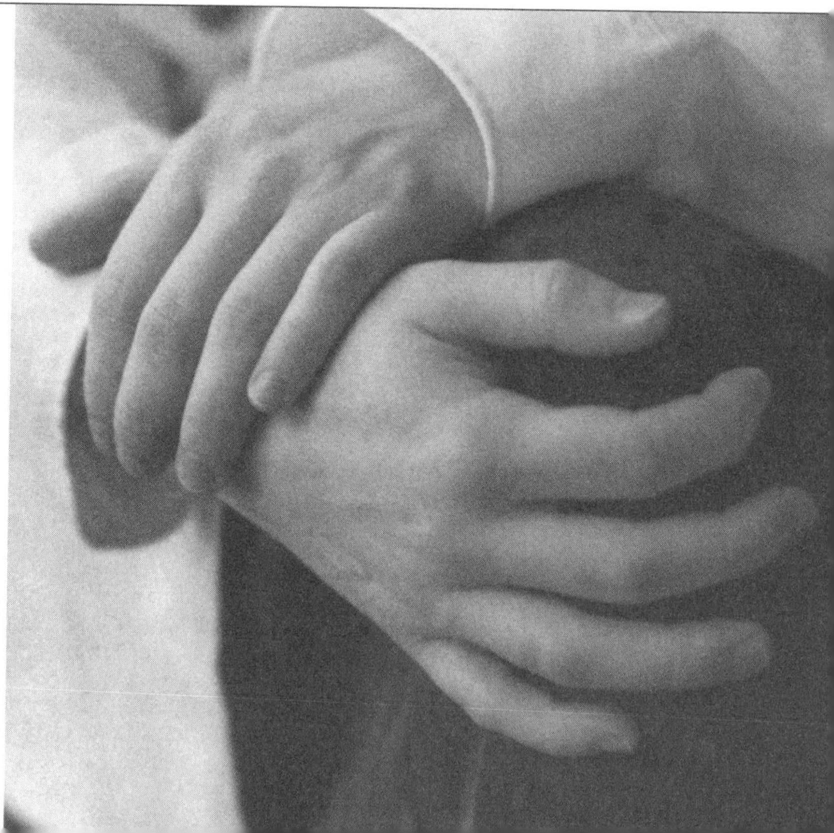

RELATING TO

Self

What we love determines what we are.

THE FIRST CHURCH OF CHRIST, SCIENTIST, AND MISCELLANY

You are not alone. Love is with
you watching tenderly over you
by day and night; and this Love
will not leave you but will sustain you and
remember all thy tears, and will
answer thy prayers.

THE MARY BAKER EDDY COLLECTION

We have nothing to fear
when Love is at the helm of thought,
but everything to enjoy on
earth and in heaven.

MISCELLANEOUS WRITINGS 1883–1896

Who that has felt the loss of human
peace has not gained stronger desires
for spiritual joy? The aspiration after
heavenly good comes even before
we discover what belongs to wisdom
and Love. The loss of earthly hopes and
pleasures brightens the ascending
path of many a heart.

SCIENCE AND HEALTH WITH KEY TO THE SCRIPTURES

May love and peace cheer your course…

THE MARY BAKER EDDY COLLECTION

Hold thought steadfastly
to the enduring, the good, and the true,
and you will bring these into your
experience proportionably to
their occupancy of your thoughts.

SCIENCE AND HEALTH WITH KEY TO THE SCRIPTURES

The measurement of life by solar years
robs youth and gives ugliness to age.

SCIENCE AND HEALTH WITH KEY TO THE SCRIPTURES

The all-engrossing care for our bodies,
the all-absorbing selfishness and
sensualism entrenched within every
form of society, betrays the greatest
ignorance of what constitutes happiness,
and the actuality of being.

THE MARY BAKER EDDY COLLECTION

All our dreams of Life in matter can
never in reality change the fact that
our life is Spirit and our body
harmonious and beautiful.

THE MARY BAKER EDDY COLLECTION

You call disease contagious
I call health contagious.

THE MARY BAKER EDDY COLLECTION

You embrace your body in your
thought, and you should delineate upon
it thoughts of health, not of sickness.

SCIENCE AND HEALTH WITH KEY TO THE SCRIPTURES

Become conscious for a single
moment that Life and intelligence are
purely spiritual, — neither in nor of matter,—
and the body will then utter no complaints.
If suffering from a belief in sickness,
you will find yourself suddenly well.
Sorrow is turned into joy when the body is
controlled by spiritual Life, Truth, and Love.

SCIENCE AND HEALTH WITH KEY TO THE SCRIPTURES

We should examine ourselves and learn
what is the affection and purpose of
the heart, for in this way only can we
learn what we honestly are.

SCIENCE AND HEALTH WITH KEY TO THE SCRIPTURES

The human heart, like a feather bed,
needs often to be *stirred*, sometimes
roughly, and given a variety of *turns*,
else it grows hard and uncomfortable
whereon to repose.

MISCELLANEOUS WRITINGS 1883–1896

We must form perfect models in
thought and look at them continually,
or we shall never carve them out in
grand and noble lives.

SCIENCE AND HEALTH WITH KEY TO THE SCRIPTURES

To live and let live, without clamor for
distinction or recognition; to wait on
divine Love; to write truth first on the
tablet of one's own heart, — this is
the sanity and perfection of living,
and my human ideal.

MESSAGE TO THE MOTHER CHURCH, 1902

Popularity, self-aggrandizement,
aught that can darken in any degree our
spirituality, must be set aside. Only
what feeds and fills the sentiment with
unworldliness, can give peace and
good will towards men.

PULPIT AND PRESS

Be honest, be true to thyself,
and true to others; then it follows
thou wilt be strong in God,
the eternal good.

RUDIMENTAL DIVINE SCIENCE

Right motives give pinions to thought,
   and strength and freedom to speech and action.

SCIENCE AND HEALTH WITH KEY TO THE SCRIPTURES

Being is holiness, harmony, immortality.
It is already proved that a knowledge of this,
even in small degree, will uplift the physical
and moral standard of mortals, will increase
longevity, will purify and elevate character.

SCIENCE AND HEALTH WITH KEY TO THE SCRIPTURES

Happiness consists in being and
in doing good; only what God gives,
and what we give ourselves and others
through His tenure, confers happiness...

MESSAGE TO THE MOTHER CHURCH, 1902

Let one's life answer well these questions,
   and it already hath a benediction:
Have you renounced self?
    Are you faithful? Do you love?

MISCELLANEOUS WRITINGS 1883–1896

RELATING TO

Others

Human affection is not poured forth
vainly, even though it meet no return.
Love enriches the nature, enlarging,
purifying, and elevating it. The wintry
blasts of earth may uproot the flowers of
affection, and scatter them to the winds;
but this severance of fleshly ties serves to
unite thought more closely to God…

SCIENCE AND HEALTH WITH KEY TO THE SCRIPTURES

Home is the dearest spot on earth,
and it should be the centre, though not
the boundary, of the affections.

SCIENCE AND HEALTH WITH KEY TO THE SCRIPTURES

Love never loses sight of loveliness.
Its halo rests upon its object. One marvels
that a friend can ever seem less
than beautiful.

SCIENCE AND HEALTH WITH KEY TO THE SCRIPTURES

There are no greater miracles known to earth
than perfection and an unbroken friendship.
We love our friends, but ofttimes we lose them
in proportion to our affection.

RETROSPECTION AND INTROSPECTION

We must love our enemies in all the manifestations wherein and whereby we love our friends; must even try not to expose their faults, but to do them good whenever opportunity occurs.

MISCELLANEOUS WRITINGS 1883–1896

Hate no one; for hatred is a plague-spot
that spreads its virus and kills at last.

MISCELLANEOUS WRITINGS 1883–1896

Hatred cannot pierce peace nor
penetrate the solid armor of Love.

THE MARY BAKER EDDY COLLECTION

Our worst enemies are the best
friends to our growth.

MISCELLANEOUS WRITINGS 1883–1896

To love, and to be loved,
one must do good to others.

MISCELLANEOUS WRITINGS 1883–1896

To disregard the welfare of others is
contrary to the law of God; therefore it
deteriorates one's ability to do good,
to benefit himself and mankind.

RETROSPECTION AND INTROSPECTION

We should measure our love for God
by our love for man...

MISCELLANEOUS WRITINGS 1883–1896

Kindred tastes, motives, and aspirations
are necessary to the formation of a
happy and permanent companionship.
The beautiful in character is also
the good, welding indissolubly
the links of affection.

SCIENCE AND HEALTH WITH KEY TO THE SCRIPTURES

Beauty, wealth, or fame is incompetent
to meet the demands of the affections,
and should never weigh against the better
claims of intellect, goodness, and virtue.

SCIENCE AND HEALTH WITH KEY TO THE SCRIPTURES

Union of the masculine and feminine
qualities constitutes completeness.
The masculine mind reaches a higher
tone through certain elements of the
feminine, while the feminine mind
gains courage and strength
through masculine qualities.

SCIENCE AND HEALTH WITH KEY TO THE SCRIPTURES

Jealousy is the grave of affection.

SCIENCE AND HEALTH WITH KEY TO THE SCRIPTURES

Be faithful over home relations;
they lead to higher joys: obey
the Golden Rule for human life,
and it will spare you much bitterness.

MISCELLANEOUS WRITINGS 1883–1896

Honesty, control over the temper,
virtue, goodness and unselfishness
make man and woman substantial…

THE MARY BAKER EDDY COLLECTION

...sympathies should blend in sweet
confidence and cheer, each partner
sustaining the other, — thus hallowing
the union of interests and affections,
in which the heart finds peace and home.

SCIENCE AND HEALTH WITH KEY TO THE SCRIPTURES

Marriage should signify a union of hearts.

SCIENCE AND HEALTH WITH KEY TO THE SCRIPTURES

A mother's affection cannot be weaned
from her child, because the mother-love
includes purity and constancy, both of
which are immortal. Therefore maternal
affection lives on under whatever difficulties.

SCIENCE AND HEALTH WITH KEY TO THE SCRIPTURES

Never contract the horizon of a worthy
outlook by the selfish exaction of
all another's time and thoughts.
With additional joys, benevolence
should grow more diffusive.

SCIENCE AND HEALTH WITH KEY TO THE SCRIPTURES

You must be just to another person
or you cannot be just to your
   own person. If you understand justice
      you will be just to yourself and others.

THE MARY BAKER EDDY COLLECTION

Wise sayings and garrulous talk may
fall to the ground, rather than on the ear
or heart of the hearer; but a tender
sentiment felt, or a kind word spoken,
at the right moment, is never wasted.

MISCELLANEOUS WRITINGS 1883–1896

When the heart speaks, however simple
the words, its language is always
acceptable to those who have hearts.

MISCELLANEOUS WRITINGS 1883–1896

The rich in spirit help the poor in one
grand brotherhood, all having the
same Principle, or Father; and blessed
is that man who seeth his brother's need
and supplieth it, seeking his own
in another's good.

SCIENCE AND HEALTH WITH KEY TO THE SCRIPTURES

CHAPTER

3

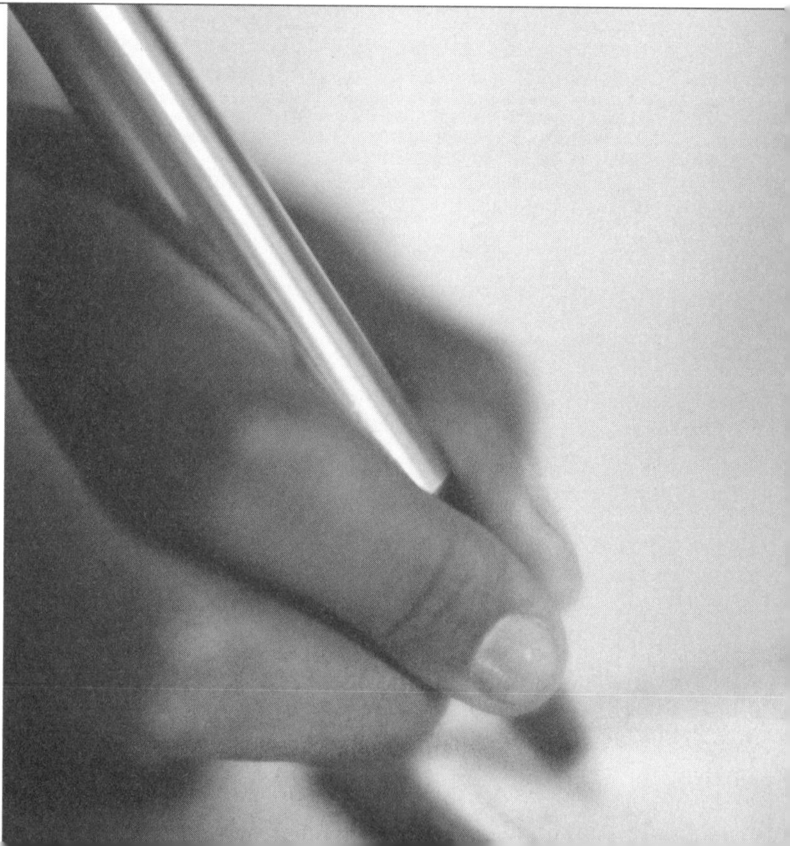

RELATING TO

Work

Success in life depends upon persistent
effort, upon the improvement of
moments more than upon any other one thing.
A great amount of time is consumed in
talking nothing, doing nothing, and indecision
as to what one should do. If one would
be successful in the future,
let him make the most of the present.

MISCELLANEOUS WRITINGS 1883–1896

There is no excellence without labor;
and the time to work, is *now*.
Only by persistent, unremitting,
straightforward toil; by turning neither
to the right nor to the left, seeking no
other pursuit or pleasure than that
which cometh from God, can you win
and wear the crown of the faithful.

MISCELLANEOUS WRITINGS 1883–1896

How would civilization have advanced
if the thinker and discoverer, the philosopher
and artisan had kept silent?

THE MARY BAKER EDDY COLLECTION

Success, prosperity and happiness follow
the footsteps of unselfed motives.

THE MARY BAKER EDDY COLLECTION

Rushing around smartly is no
proof of accomplishing much.

MISCELLANEOUS WRITINGS 1883–1896

Mind is not necessarily dependent upon
educational processes. It possesses of
itself all beauty and poetry, and the power
of expressing them. Spirit, God, is heard
when the senses are silent. We are all
capable of more than we do.

SCIENCE AND HEALTH WITH KEY TO THE SCRIPTURES

It is proverbial that Florence Nightingale
and other philanthropists engaged in
humane labors have been able to
undergo without sinking fatigues and
exposures which ordinary people could
not endure. The explanation lies in the
support which they derived from the
divine law, rising above the human.

SCIENCE AND HEALTH WITH KEY TO THE SCRIPTURES

The true leader of a true cause is the unacknowledged servant of mankind. Stationary in the background, this individual is doing the work that nobody else can or will do. An erratic career is like the comet's course, dashing through space, headlong and alone.

MISCELLANEOUS WRITINGS 1883–1896

One must fulfil one's mission without timidity or dissimulation, for to be well done, the work must be done unselfishly.

SCIENCE AND HEALTH WITH KEY TO THE SCRIPTURES

The lives of great men and women are
miracles of patience and perseverance.

MISCELLANEOUS WRITINGS 1883–1896

…to understand God is the work of eternity,
and demands absolute consecration of
thought, energy, and desire.

SCIENCE AND HEALTH WITH KEY TO THE SCRIPTURES

Spirit, God, gathers unformed thoughts
into their proper channels, and unfolds
these thoughts, even as He opens the
petals of a holy purpose in order that
the purpose may appear.

SCIENCE AND HEALTH WITH KEY TO THE SCRIPTURES

Each successive stage of experience
　　　unfolds new views of divine
goodness and love.

SCIENCE AND HEALTH WITH KEY TO THE SCRIPTURES

CHAPTER

4

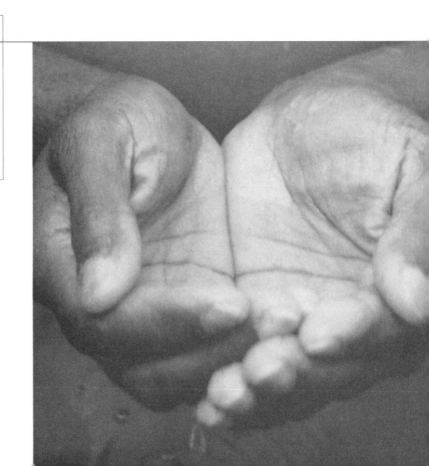

RELATING TO THE

World

Have you ever pictured this heaven
and earth, inhabited by beings under
the control of supreme wisdom?

SCIENCE AND HEALTH WITH KEY TO THE SCRIPTURES

…our ideas of divinity form our
models of humanity.

THE PEOPLE'S IDEA OF GOD

Eternal Truth is changing the universe.
As mortals drop off their mental
swaddling-clothes, thought expands
into expression. "Let there be light," is the
perpetual demand of Truth and Love,
changing chaos into order and discord
into the music of the spheres.

SCIENCE AND HEALTH WITH KEY TO THE SCRIPTURES

Love, redolent with unselfishness, bathes all in beauty and light. The grass beneath our feet silently exclaims, "The meek shall inherit the earth." The modest arbutus sends her sweet breath to heaven. The great rock gives shadow and shelter. The sunlight glints from the church-dome, glances into the prison-cell, glides into the sick-chamber, brightens the flower, beautifies the landscape, blesses the earth.

SCIENCE AND HEALTH WITH KEY TO THE SCRIPTURES

I will not attempt to convey by words
a picture of the magnificence of the visible
universe. The effort would be futile
and yet the whole scene is only the
picture of ideas; the imagery of thought;
the hieroglyphic record of the act;
and meditation of Deity.

THE MARY BAKER EDDY COLLECTION

The substance of God's love touches us
through the order of nature, the harmonies
of space, the smile of the flowers,
the peace of the plains, the pomp
of mountains, the mirror of the morn
but this love reaches us nearer and touches
us more divinely apart from the eye,
in the silent consecration of our affections,
hopes and joys, in illumined secrecy in
a quickened sense of the divine love
Life's only recompense.

THE MARY BAKER EDDY COLLECTION

The world is filled with spectral men
and women, with lean hazy minds,
getting more unsubstantial every day, — by
means of their materialism. We see it in the
common aims of life, in the misguided
ambition of popular sentiment, in the temper
of the market, the injustice of the press…

THE MARY BAKER EDDY COLLECTION

Take away wealth, fame, and social
organizations, which weigh not one jot
in the balance of God, and we get clearer
views of Principle. Break up cliques,
level wealth with honesty, let worth be
judged according to wisdom, and we get
better views of humanity.

SCIENCE AND HEALTH WITH KEY TO THE SCRIPTURES

The few who leave behind an earthly
record, are they, who have brought to
human consciousness a higher sense
of substance, have defined existence
more *spiritually* and happiness
more *unselfishly*.

THE MARY BAKER EDDY COLLECTION

From lack of moral strength
empires fall.
Right alone is irresistible,
permanent, eternal.

MISCELLANEOUS WRITINGS 1883–1896

If we look back upon the nations
that have ruled the world, we shall learn
how impotent are all the material implements
and appliances of power, if there be not
a groundwork of right, a spiritual strength,
for the support of greatness.

THE MARY BAKER EDDY COLLECTION

History gives startling records of the
transient nature of all systems civil,
political or religious not based on right
foundations. And the right has always
rested on the spirituality of those
foundations and their superstructures and
has advanced accordingly as each have
risen above the material method to one
more spiritual and taken a basis in the
higher motives and affections of man.

THE MARY BAKER EDDY COLLECTION

…unite in prayer for peace: For the end
of hostility and war among or between
all nations, and religious sects, — for divine
Love to make us one human family, to
have one Father-Mother God, one Christ,
whereof the Scriptures bear witness; and
to demonstrate the divine Life, Truth, and
Love — healing the sick, blessing our enemies,
and all mankind.

THE MARY BAKER EDDY COLLECTION

To suppose that God constitutes laws of
inharmony is a mistake; discords have no
support from nature or divine law,
however much is said to the contrary.

SCIENCE AND HEALTH WITH KEY TO THE SCRIPTURES

Whatever change belongs to this century,
or any epoch, we may safely submit to the
providence of God, to common justice,
individual rights and governmental usages.

THE MARY BAKER EDDY COLLECTION

Let Truth uncover and destroy error
in God's own way, and let human justice
pattern the divine. Sin will receive
its full penalty, both for what it is
and for what it does.

SCIENCE AND HEALTH WITH KEY TO THE SCRIPTURES

There should be painless progress,
attended by life and peace instead
of discord and death.

SCIENCE AND HEALTH WITH KEY TO THE SCRIPTURES

Pray for the prosperity of our country,
and for her victory under arms;
that justice, mercy, and peace continue
to characterize her government,
and that they shall rule all nations.

CHRISTIAN SCIENCE VERSUS PANTHEISM

Enable us to know, — as in heaven,
    so on earth, — God is omnipotent, supreme.

SCIENCE AND HEALTH WITH KEY TO THE SCRIPTURES

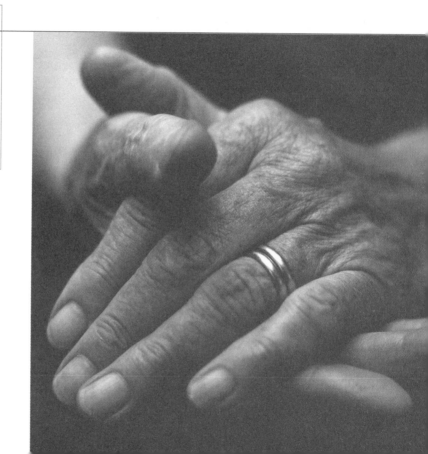

RELATING TO

God

God is universal;
        confined to no spot,
defined by no dogma,
        appropriated by no sect.

MISCELLANEOUS WRITINGS 1883–1896

God is Love. Can we ask Him to be more?
God is intelligence. Can we inform the
infinite Mind of anything He does not
already comprehend? Do we expect to
change perfection? Shall we plead for
more at the open fount, which is pouring
forth more than we accept?

SCIENCE AND HEALTH WITH KEY TO THE SCRIPTURES

Divine Love always has met and
always will meet every human need.

SCIENCE AND HEALTH WITH KEY TO THE SCRIPTURES

Take courage. God is leading
you onward and upward.

THE FIRST CHURCH OF CHRIST, SCIENTIST, AND MISCELLANY

Spirit, God, gathers unformed thoughts
into their proper channels, and unfolds
these thoughts, even as He opens the
petals of a holy purpose in order that
the purpose may appear.

SCIENCE AND HEALTH WITH KEY TO THE SCRIPTURES

Love giveth to the least spiritual idea
might, immortality, and goodness,
which shine through all as the blossom
shines through the bud. All the
varied expressions of God reflect health,
holiness, immortality — infinite
Life, Truth, and Love.

SCIENCE AND HEALTH WITH KEY TO THE SCRIPTURES

God expresses in man the infinite idea
forever developing itself, broadening
and rising higher and higher from a
boundless basis.

SCIENCE AND HEALTH WITH KEY TO THE SCRIPTURES

Simply asking that we may love God
will never make us love Him;
but the longing to be better and holier,
expressed in daily watchfulness and
in striving to assimilate more of the
divine character, will mould and fashion
us anew, until we awake in His likeness.

SCIENCE AND HEALTH WITH KEY TO THE SCRIPTURES

Practice not profession, understanding
not belief, gain the ear and right hand
of omnipotence and they assuredly
call down infinite blessings.

SCIENCE AND HEALTH WITH KEY TO THE SCRIPTURES

Spiritual sense is a conscious,
   constant capacity to understand God.

SCIENCE AND HEALTH WITH KEY TO THE SCRIPTURES

Thoughts unspoken are not unknown
to the divine Mind. Desire is prayer; and
no loss can occur from trusting God
with our desires, that they may be
molded and exalted before they take
form in words and in deeds.

SCIENCE AND HEALTH WITH KEY TO THE SCRIPTURES

As our ideas of Deity become
more spiritual, we express them by
objects more beautiful.

THE PEOPLE'S IDEA OF GOD

To me God is All. He is best understood
as Supreme Being, as infinite and
conscious Life, as the affectionate
Father and Mother of all He creates...

UNITY OF GOOD

That which reflects order, beauty
and good, in thought, action or object,
hath Immortality.

THE MARY BAKER EDDY COLLECTION

The time for thinkers has come. Truth,
   independent of doctrines and time-honored
systems, knocks at the portal of humanity.
   Contentment with the past and the cold
conventionality of materialism are
      crumbling away. Ignorance of God
      is no longer the steppingstone to faith.
The only guarantee of obedience is a right
   apprehension of Him whom to know
aright is Life eternal. Though empires fall,
      "the Lord shall reign forever."

SCIENCE AND HEALTH WITH KEY TO THE SCRIPTURES

Spirit blesses man, but man cannot "tell whence it cometh." By it the sick are healed, the sorrowing are comforted, and the sinning are reformed.

SCIENCE AND HEALTH WITH KEY TO THE SCRIPTURES

Let us be patient, God governs
to-day and tomorrow.

THE MARY BAKER EDDY COLLECTION

To those leaning on the sustaining infinite,
to-day is big with blessings.

SCIENCE AND HEALTH WITH KEY TO THE SCRIPTURES

www.spirituality.com is based on the ideas in Mary Baker Eddy's bestselling work, *Science and Health with Key to the Scriptures*. Articles, features, discussion boards, and live round-table chats explore spirituality in relation to careers, finance, self/identity, wellness, relationships, and more.

On spirituality.com you will also find features inspired by this book.
Visit www.spirituality.com/lifesrelationships to:

- discuss the book
- post a quote that inspires you
- tell your story
- send an e-card
- write your own quote about life's relationships

www.marybakereddylibrary.org offers an in-depth look at Mary Baker Eddy's life and legacy. The Mary Baker Eddy Library for the Betterment of Humanity houses The Mary Baker Eddy Collection™ — one of the largest by and about an American woman — which includes thousands of pages of her letters, diaries, and manuscripts, as well as photographs, and artifacts. The website features upcoming events, forums, research programs, summer institutes, and online exhibits, all inspired by Mary Baker Eddy's timeless ideas and life of achievement.

* *Science and Health* *

Science and Health with Key to the Scriptures by Mary Baker Eddy has been improving the health and changing the lives of millions of readers around the world for over 125 years. Today it remains one of the most enduring books on spirituality and healing and was chosen as one of 75 books by women whose words have changed the world (Women's National Book Association).

Science and Health can be purchased online at spirituality.com and at bookstores and Christian Science Reading Rooms worldwide.

* *photo credits* *

COVER
Left — photo by Jen Fong
Middle — photo by Johner
Right — photo by Antony Nagelmann

RELATING TO SELF, page 10
Photography by Mel Curtis, Getty/PhotoDisc

RELATING TO OTHERS, page 34
Photography by Jen Fong, Photonica

RELATING TO WORK, page 60
Photography by Antony Nagelmann, Getty/Taxi

RELATING TO THE WORLD, page 74
Photography by Patrick Molner, Getty/Stone

RELATING TO GOD, page 94
Photography by Johner, Photonica